THE TOP TEN
EXPLORERS & PIONEERS
THAT CHANGED THE WORLD

Anita Ganeri

PowerKiDS press.

New York

D0841293

Published in 2010 by The Rosen Publishing Group, Inc.
29 East 21st Street, New York 10010

Designed and produced by
David West Books

Designer: Gary Jeffrey
Illustrator: David West
Editor: Katharine Pethick
U.S. Editor: Kara Murray

Photographic credits: 6, 7tr, Matt Celeskey; 7bl, Shaun Che; 15ml, 15br, NOAA; 24-25 all images courtesy of NASA except 25mr, ideonexus o; 29bl, cliff1066; 29, NOAA; 29br, NASA

Library of Congress Cataloging-in-Publication Data

Ganeri, Anita, 1961–
The top ten explorers & pioneers that changed the world / Anita Ganeri.
p. cm. — (Top ten)
Includes index.
ISBN 978-1-4358-9167-8 (library binding) — ISBN 978-1-4358-9168-5 (pbk.) —
ISBN 978-1-4358-9169-2 (6-pack)
1. Explorers—Juvenile literature. 2. Discoveries in geography—Juvenile literature. I. Title.
G175.G37 2010
910.92'2—dc22

2009019514

Printed in China

Contents

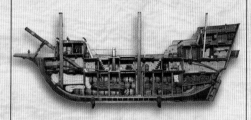
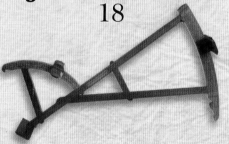

Introduction

The following stories of explorers and pioneers have been selected as the top ten from hundreds of others that have also changed our world. So why have we chosen these ten explorers and why these particular journeys?

✳ First, the exploration must have had an impact on the entire world, not just a part of it.

✳ Second, it must have been a genuine voyage of exploration, rather than simply of mapmaking or conquest.

The sixteenth-century Dutch mapmaker Gerardus Mercator contributed to knowledge of geography but did not explore.

Lewis and Clark's expedition mostly affected America, not the whole world.

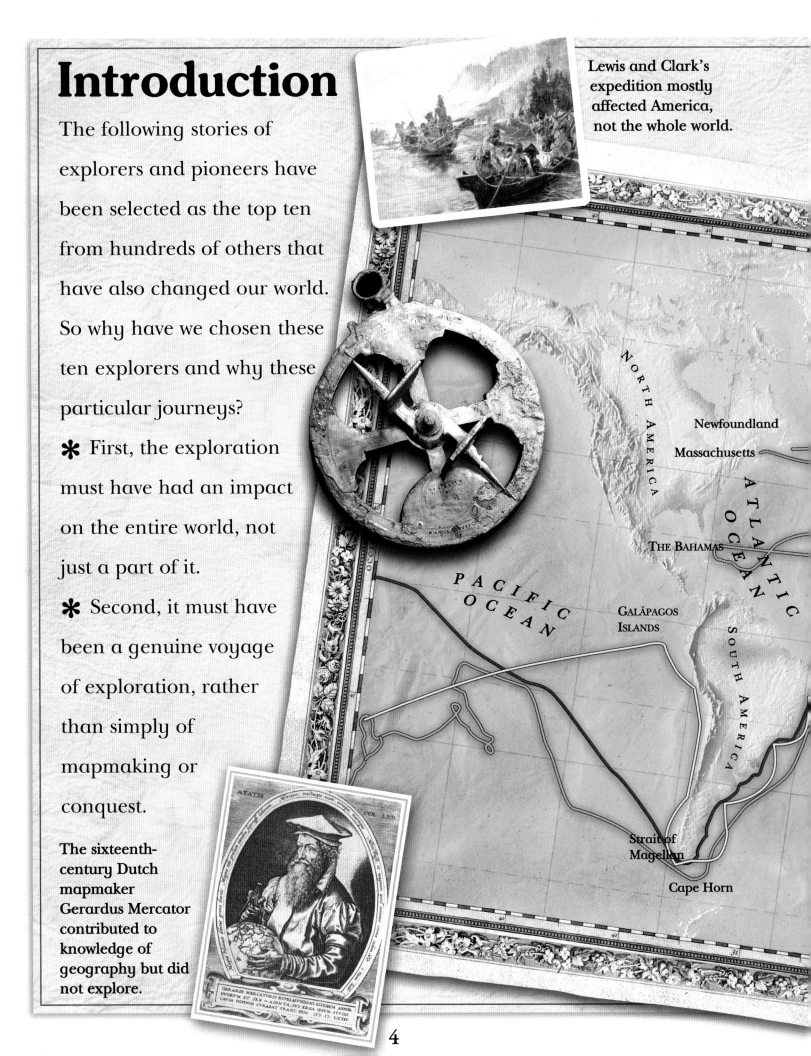

NORTH AMERICA

Newfoundland

Massachusetts

ATLANTIC OCEAN

THE BAHAMAS

PACIFIC OCEAN

GALÁPAGOS ISLANDS

SOUTH AMERICA

Strait of Magellan

Cape Horn

4

* Third, the exploration must have been led by an adventurer or small group of people, rather than a company. (Expeditions led by trading companies have been excluded.) You might disagree with the explorers that were picked for this list. If so, you might like to make your own list of important explorers.

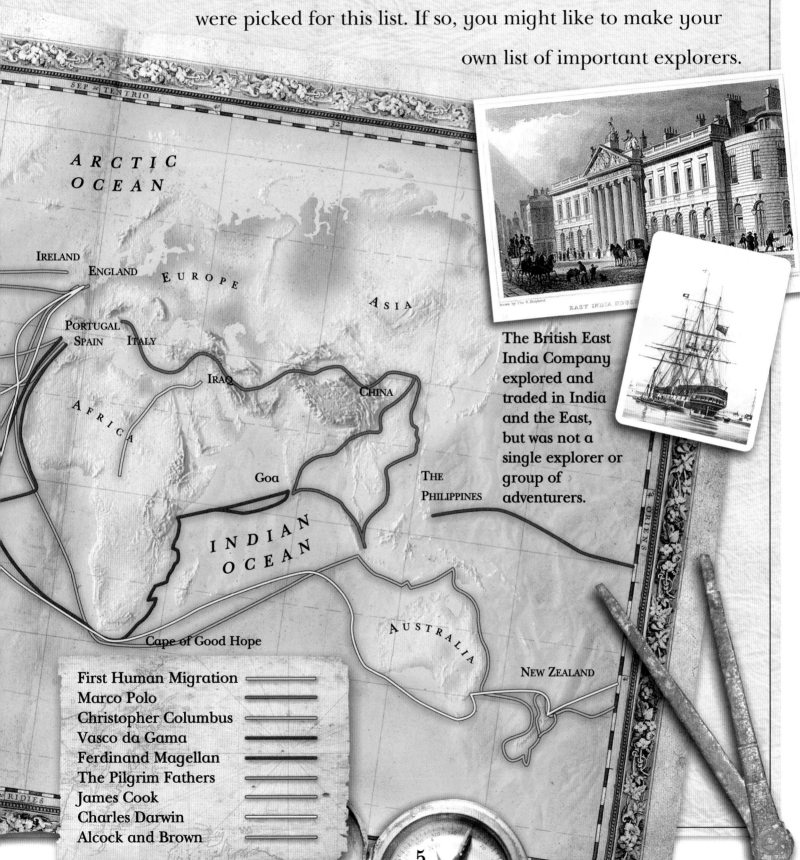

The British East India Company explored and traded in India and the East, but was not a single explorer or group of adventurers.

First Human Migration
Marco Polo
Christopher Columbus
Vasco da Gama
Ferdinand Magellan
The Pilgrim Fathers
James Cook
Charles Darwin
Alcock and Brown

The First Human Migration

The story of exploration begins hundreds of thousands of years ago. It is widely believed that the ancestors of modern humans (*Homo sapiens*) evolved in Africa around 200,000 years ago. This is the only place where their remains have been found. They lived a nomadic lifestyle, moving from place to place in search of food. Then, around 70,000 years ago, possibly because of a lack of food or a changing climate, some of these early humans began to explore the land northeast of Africa, crossing into the Middle East. By 40,000 years ago, early humans had reached as far as Asia, Australia, and Europe.

An earlier hominin, *Homo erectus,* also made long journeys.

FIRST OF MANY

Early humans found food by hunting animals and gathering wild plants to eat. Around 10,000 B.C., in a part of the Middle East known as the Fertile Crescent (modern-day Turkey, Syria, Iran, and Iraq), people developed a more settled way of life based on farming. Once people began to cultivate crops, they began to settle in one place and build early towns, such as Catal Huyuk in Turkey. The earliest civilizations developed on the fertile land around the Tigris River and Euphrates River in Mesopotamia. In the years since early humans left Africa, the world had changed forever.

As they spread, *Homo sapiens* replaced other hominins, such as Neanderthals.

Stones used by early farmers for grinding grain to make flour

The first civilizations rose in the land between the Tigris and Euphrates.

A Sumerian clay writing tablet from around 2400 B.C.

A Mesopotamian worship figure carved nearly 5,000 years ago

Marco Polo

Marco Polo (1254–1324)

In May 1275, three weary travelers arrived at the summer palace of the great Kublai Khan in Shangdu, China. They were brothers, Nicolo and Maffeo Polo, two jewel merchants from Venice, and Nicolo's 20-year-old son, Marco. Their journey from Italy had taken three and a half years, following dangerous trade routes across high mountains and blazing deserts. The khan welcomed the Polos warmly and was particularly impressed by young Marco, who was dazzled by the splendors of the court.

Nicolo and Maffeo had met Kublai Khan before. In 1260, they were among the first Europeans to set off for China. They returned to Venice nine years later, having successfully sold their entire stock of jewels.

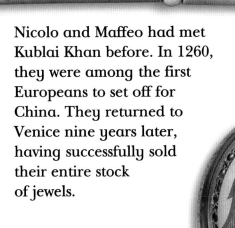

The Chinese emperor Kublai Khan was the grandson of Genghis Khan.

WEST MEETS EAST

Marco spent the next 17 years in China, employed by Kublai Khan as an envoy of the imperial court. During this time, he visited many parts of the empire and saw many extraordinary sights. These included paper money, printed books and fireworks, unknown in Europe at that time. In 1292, the Polos finally left for home, reaching Venice in 1295. Three years later, Marco was captured fighting for his city against the Genoese. In prison, he told his story to a writer named Rusticello. *The Travels of Marco Polo* became one of the most famous travel books of all time, inspiring many future explorers, including Christopher Columbus.

An illustration from Marco Polo's *Travels*

By the eleventh century, paper money was used regularly in China.

Many of the names on Frau Mauro's fifteenth-century map come from the writings of Marco Polo.

Columbus made notes in his copy of Marco Polo's book.

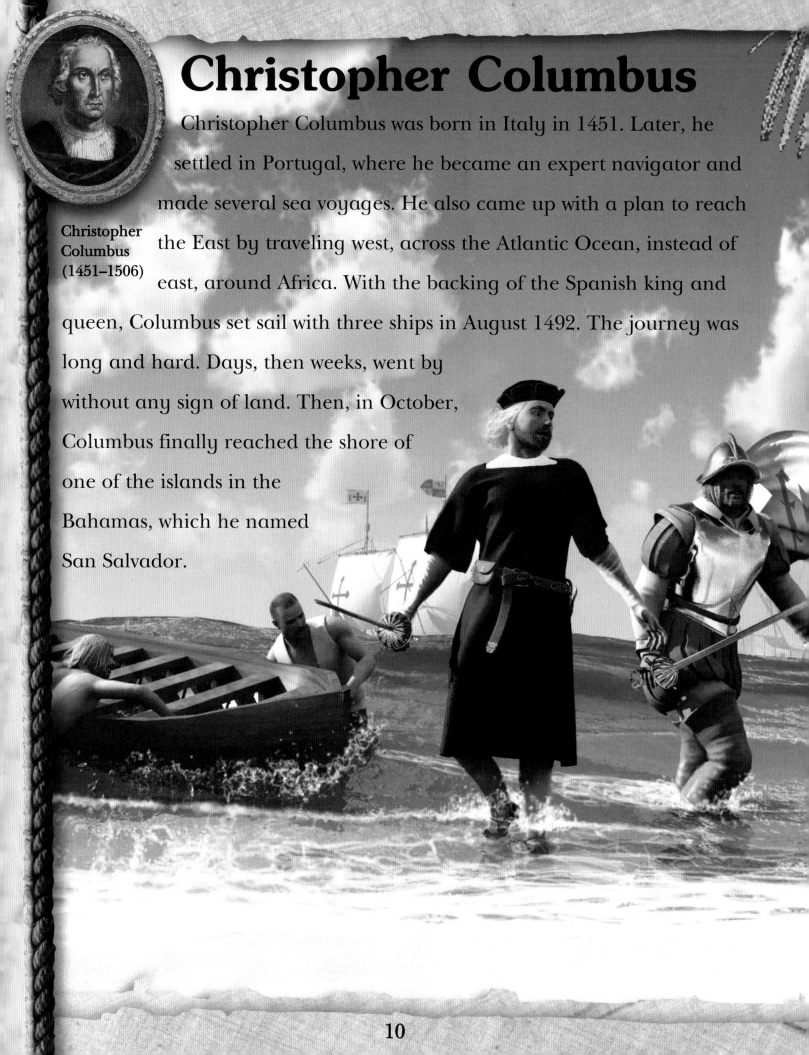

Christopher Columbus

Christopher Columbus was born in Italy in 1451. Later, he settled in Portugal, where he became an expert navigator and made several sea voyages. He also came up with a plan to reach the East by traveling west, across the Atlantic Ocean, instead of east, around Africa. With the backing of the Spanish king and queen, Columbus set sail with three ships in August 1492. The journey was long and hard. Days, then weeks, went by without any sign of land. Then, in October, Columbus finally reached the shore of one of the islands in the Bahamas, which he named San Salvador.

Christopher
Columbus
(1451–1506)

A MAGNIFICENT FAILURE

Columbus claimed the island for Spain. From there, he went on to explore Cuba and Hispaniola (the modern-day Dominican Republic and Haiti). Back home in Spain, he was given a hero's welcome and made governor of the new lands. To his dying day, however, Columbus remained convinced that the islands he had reached lay off the coast of China. He greatly underestimated the circumference of Earth, and had no idea that any land lay between Europe and Asia. In fact, his voyages opened up the "New World" of the Americas, changing our understanding of the world.

Columbus used this map, made in 1490, to chart his first voyage.

Explorers of the New World brought many unkown products back to Europe, such as pineapples, potatoes, and tobacco.

The first Europeans to visit the New World were Vikings around A.D. 1,000.

The indigenous peoples of the Americas were treated very badly by European explorers. Many were enslaved, killed, or died from disease.

America was named after another Italian explorer, Amerigo Vespucci. He sailed to the New World in 1499 and made many maps of the continents he explored.

11

Vasco da Gama

Vasco da Gama
(1460–1524)

In July 1497, Portuguese navigator Vasco da Gama set sail from Lisbon with four ships and 170 men. His mission was to find a new trade route around Africa to the riches of the East. Several expeditions had already tried to sail this way and failed. Now, it was da Gama's turn to sail into the unknown.

To take advantage of favorable winds, da Gama set out deep into the Atlantic Ocean, instead of hugging the coast. It was risky, but successful, and he reached the Cape of Good Hope by November. From there, he sailed up the east coast of Africa and out across the Indian Ocean. In May 1498, his fleet finally reached India.

In da Gama's time, Calicut on the west coast of India was the major port for all of southern India. However, the Portuguese would have to fight Arab merchants for control of trade.

SEAFARERS

For decades before da Gama, Portuguese sailors had undertaken ocean voyages in search of trade routes to the valuable spice markets of the East. Many were sent by Prince Henry the Navigator, who trained navigators and pilots at his school in southern Portugal. Henry's expeditions paved the way for da Gama's historic voyage. A few years later, Pedro Alvares Cabral accidentally reached Brazil and claimed it for Portugal. A golden age of exploration and expansion had begun.

In 1488, Portuguese navigator Bartolomeu Dias rounded the Cape of Good Hope.

Pedro Alvares Cabral (1647–1520)

A sixteenth-century map showing the Portuguese colony of Brazil

Prince Henry the Navigator (1394–1460) was the driving force behind Portuguese exploration.

This is a Portuguese caravel. It was a new type of sailing ship.

An eighteenth-century Portuguese coin minted in India

Ferdinand Magellan

Ferdinand Magellan (1480–1521)

In September 1519, Portuguese aristocrat and adventurer Ferdinand Magellan embarked on one of the most daring sea voyages ever. Backed by the king of Spain, his aim was to reach the spice islands of the East by sailing west, around South America, instead of east, around Africa.

Magellan left Spain with five ships and about 270 men. Crossing the Atlantic Ocean, he headed for Brazil and down the east coast of South America. Finally, a year after setting sail from Spain, Magellan sailed through a narrow passage (later named the Strait of Magellan, after him) and out into the Pacific Ocean.

MAGELLAN'S ODYSSEY

Crossing the Pacific Ocean was very difficult. For 98 days, Magellan saw no land, apart from two small islands. By now, supplies were running dangerously low. The starving men had only old, moldy biscuits to eat. Several men died from scurvy. Magellan reached Guam in March 1521, then sailed on to the Philippines, where he was killed in a fight. Juan Sebastian del Cano took command of the ship. In September 1522, the *Victoria* limped back to Spain alone, with only 18 men left alive. The first circumnavigation of the world had been achieved but at a very high price.

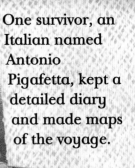

One survivor, an Italian named Antonio Pigafetta, kept a detailed diary and made maps of the voyage.

Pigafetta's map of the Strait of Magellan

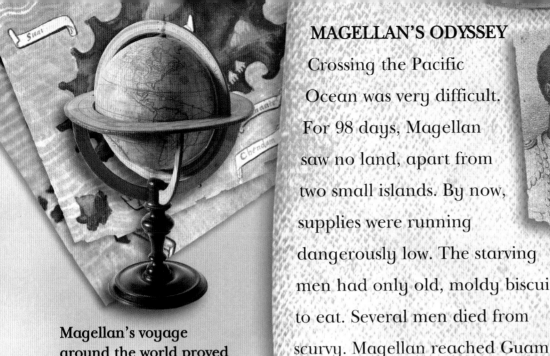

Magellan's voyage around the world proved that the Earth was round.

Sailors used a tool called a cross staff to figure out a ship's latitude.

Magellan and his men had only basic navigational tools.

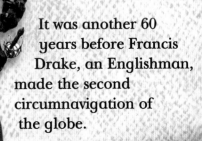

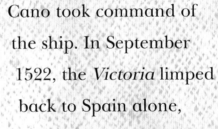

A Magellan penguin

It was another 60 years before Francis Drake, an Englishman, made the second circumnavigation of the globe.

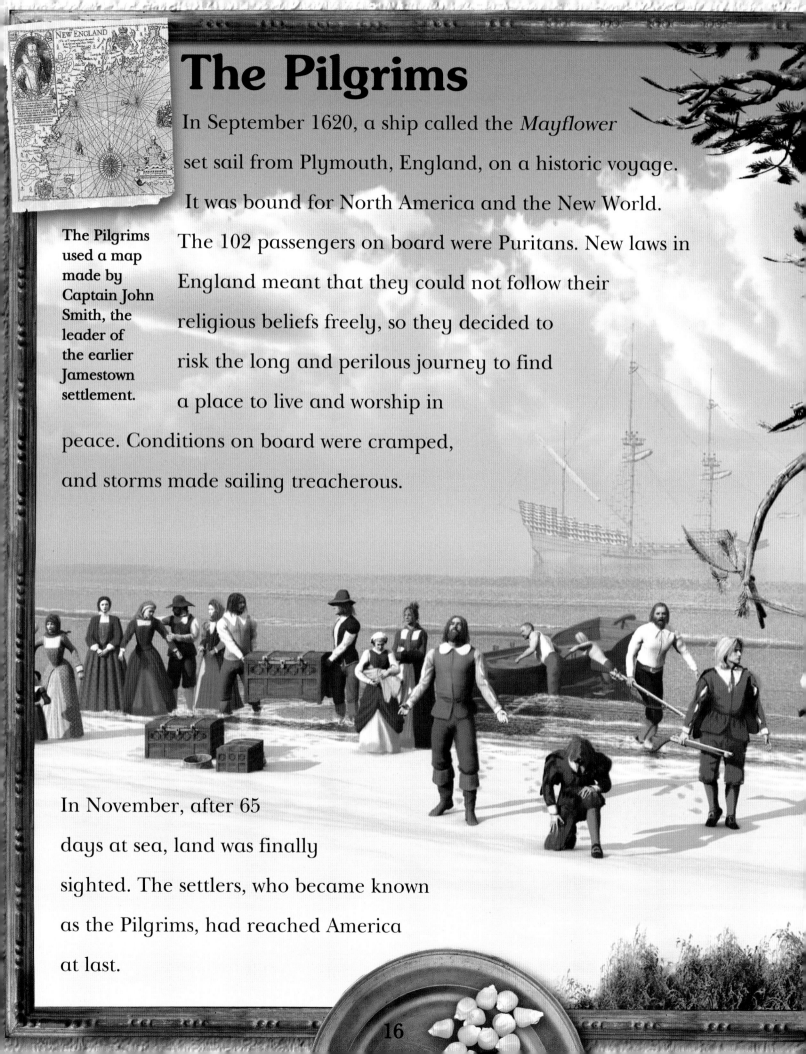

The Pilgrims

In September 1620, a ship called the *Mayflower* set sail from Plymouth, England, on a historic voyage. It was bound for North America and the New World.

The 102 passengers on board were Puritans. New laws in England meant that they could not follow their religious beliefs freely, so they decided to risk the long and perilous journey to find a place to live and worship in peace. Conditions on board were cramped, and storms made sailing treacherous.

The Pilgrims used a map made by Captain John Smith, the leader of the earlier Jamestown settlement.

In November, after 65 days at sea, land was finally sighted. The settlers, who became known as the Pilgrims, had reached America at last.

ENGLISH COLONIES

The settlers landed near Cape Cod, on the East Coast of America. Nearby, they founded a small settlement, which they named Plymouth. However, their first winter in their new home proved tragically tough. The weather was

The Plymouth settlers mostly avoided the conflict with the local Native Americans that had set back the earlier English colonists in Jamestown, Virginia.

freezing, food ran low, and many of the settlers got sick. Within a few months, almost half of them had died. With the help of the local Native Americans, however, the settlers learned to farm and fish and the colony grew. Over the next 100 years,

A cross section of a merchant ship, similar to the *Mayflower*

more settlers followed from England, establishing their own colonies. The 13 original English colonies later became the first 13 states of the United States of America.

The Mayflower Compact was the first set of rules for the Plymouth Colony.

John Carver was elected the first governor of the Plymouth Colony. Here, he meets local Native American leaders.

James Cook

Born in the port of Whitby, England, James Cook learned to sail on a coal ship. He later joined the Royal British Navy and was quickly promoted up through the ranks. Then, in 1768, he was chosen to command an important scientific voyage to the Pacific Ocean. First, Cook headed for the island of Tahiti to observe the passage of the planet Venus in front of the Sun. However, he had also been given a secret mission. Cook was told to sail even further south to discover the mysterious "southern continent." Although Cook did not see Antarctica, he visited both New Zealand and Australia before finally returning home in 1771.

James Cook
(1728–1779)

BRETON I.

This 1598 map of the world shows a huge continent, known as *Terra Australis* (Southern Land).

THE REMARKABLE VOYAGES OF CAPTAIN COOK

On his first voyage, Cook charted vast areas of the Pacific Ocean and brought back valuable information about the people and places he had seen. On his second voyage (1772–1775), he crossed the Antarctic Circle twice and narrowly missed seeing Antarctica.

On his third voyage (1776–1779), he discovered the islands of Hawaii, where he later died. As well as being a fine sailor, Cook was also ahead of his time in the care he took of his men's health. When possible, he made sure that they ate fresh food to ward off scurvy. His voyages were remarkable feats of navigation, mapmaking, and scientific discovery.

Cook's crew were the first Europeans to see an Australian kangaroo.

HMS *Resolution* was the first ship to cross the Antarctic Circle, in 1773.

A breadfruit

Cook did not complete his third voyage. He was killed on a beach in Hawaii during a quarrel over a stolen boat.

Cook made use of the latest technology, taking a chronometer like this one on his second voyage.

Charles Darwin

Charles Darwin (1809–1882)

In 1831, British naturalist Charles Darwin joined a ship called HMS *Beagle* on a five-year voyage to South America that would change Darwin's life. As the crew surveyed and charted the coastline, Darwin made detailed notes of everything he saw and built up a huge collection of fossils, rocks, plants, and animals in his tiny cabin. In September 1835, the *Beagle* reached the Galápagos Islands, off the coast of Ecuador in the Pacific Ocean. There, Darwin noticed that animals and plants of the same species living on different islands had developed slightly different features.

Darwin saw that the shapes of the shells of the Galápagos giant tortoises differed slightly from island to island.

1. Geospiza magnirostris.
2. Geospiza fortis.
3. Geospiza parvula.
4. Certhidea olivacea.

The specialized beak shapes of the Galápagos finches (above) and the discovery of a new species of rhea (right) in South America made Darwin think about natural selection.

THE BIG ANSWER

The *Beagle* reached England in October 1836 and Darwin spent the next 20 years writing up his findings. He realized that different features helped plants and animals adapt to life in their particular habitats. For example, each island's finches had beaks suited to a particular type of food. These helpful adaptations were passed on to the next generation to help them survive. Darwin called this process natural selection and believed it to be the driving force behind evolution. In 1859, Darwin published a book, called *On the Origin of Species by Means of Natural Selection,* which explained his ground-breaking theory.

Darwin was ridiculed for his ideas, which went against the teachings of Christianity.

Many important Victorian scientists, including Thomas Huxley, supported Darwin's cause.

Darwin's theory was that all living things had evolved over millions of years and that early hominins were the ancestors of present-day humans.

ON
THE ORIGIN OF SPECIES
BY MEANS OF NATURAL SELECTION,

The Origin of Species is widely considered to be one of the most important books of all time.

John Alcock (1892–1919) and Arthur Whitten Brown (1886–1948)

Alcock and Brown

In 1918, the *Daily Mail* newspaper offered a prize of 10,000 British pounds to the first person to fly across the Atlantic Ocean, between North America and Britain, in under 72 hours. British airmen John Alcock and Arthur Whitten Brown took up the challenge. At around 1:45 p.m. on June 14, 1919, they took off from Newfoundland, Canada, in their Vickers Vimy IV aircraft. The next day, they crashed into a muddy field in Ireland. They had covered the 1,888 miles (3,040 km) in 16 hours and 27 minutes. The prize was theirs. However, it had not been an easy flight. Had it not been for the men's superb flying skills, their trip could easily have ended in disaster.

Fog, snow, and ice had made flying conditions very dangerous and the aircraft was badly damaged.

INTO THE BLUE YONDER

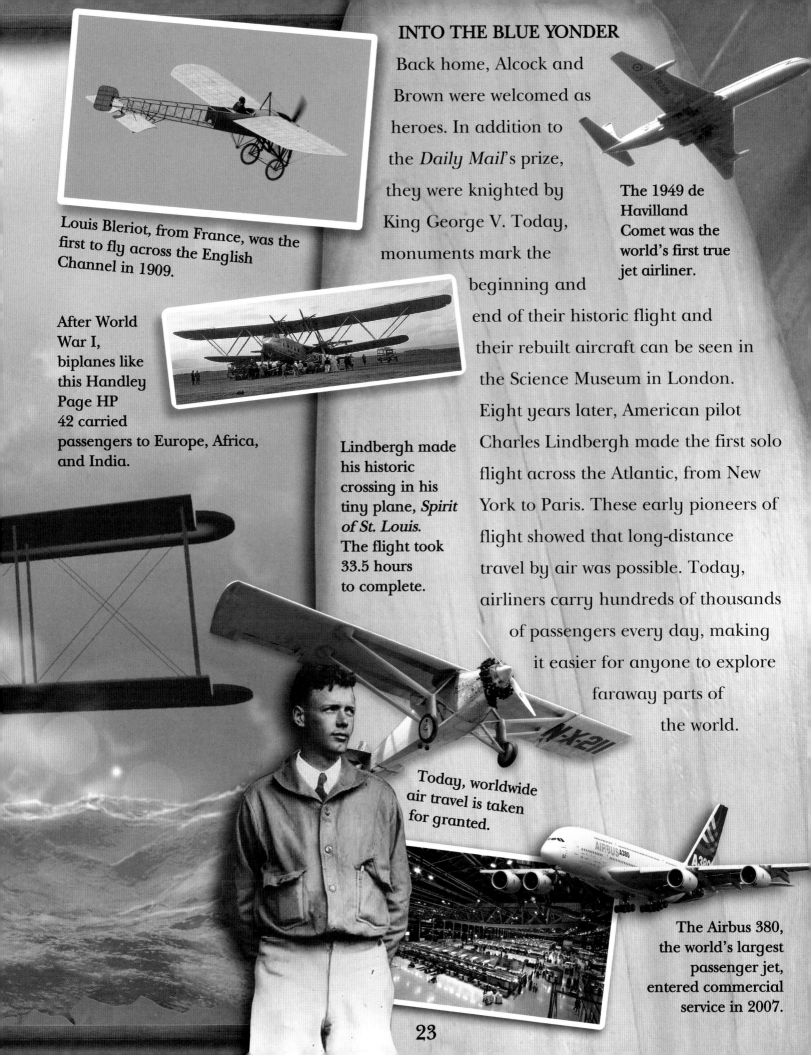

Louis Bleriot, from France, was the first to fly across the English Channel in 1909.

After World War I, biplanes like this Handley Page HP 42 carried passengers to Europe, Africa, and India.

Lindbergh made his historic crossing in his tiny plane, *Spirit of St. Louis*. The flight took 33.5 hours to complete.

Back home, Alcock and Brown were welcomed as heroes. In addition to the *Daily Mail*'s prize, they were knighted by King George V. Today, monuments mark the beginning and end of their historic flight and their rebuilt aircraft can be seen in the Science Museum in London. Eight years later, American pilot Charles Lindbergh made the first solo flight across the Atlantic, from New York to Paris. These early pioneers of flight showed that long-distance travel by air was possible. Today, airliners carry hundreds of thousands of passengers every day, making it easier for anyone to explore faraway parts of the world.

The 1949 de Havilland Comet was the world's first true jet airliner.

Today, worldwide air travel is taken for granted.

The Airbus 380, the world's largest passenger jet, entered commercial service in 2007.

23

Yuri Gagarin

Yuri Gagarin (1934–1968)

Born in Russia in 1934, Yuri Gagarin learned to fly airplanes at his local flying club and later joined the Soviet Air Force. In 1959, he was interviewed for a "special project," to train as a cosmonaut. Gagarin excelled in his training and, in April 1961, was selected to be the pilot of *Vostok I*, the first manned spacecraft. On April 12, Gagarin became the first person ever to fly in space. In a flight lasting for 108 minutes, he made a single orbit of Earth, traveling at a speed of 28,000 miles per hour (45,000 km/h).

After his flight, Gagarin ejected from the *Vostok* capsule about 4.5 miles (7 km) above the ground and parachuted safely back down to Earth.

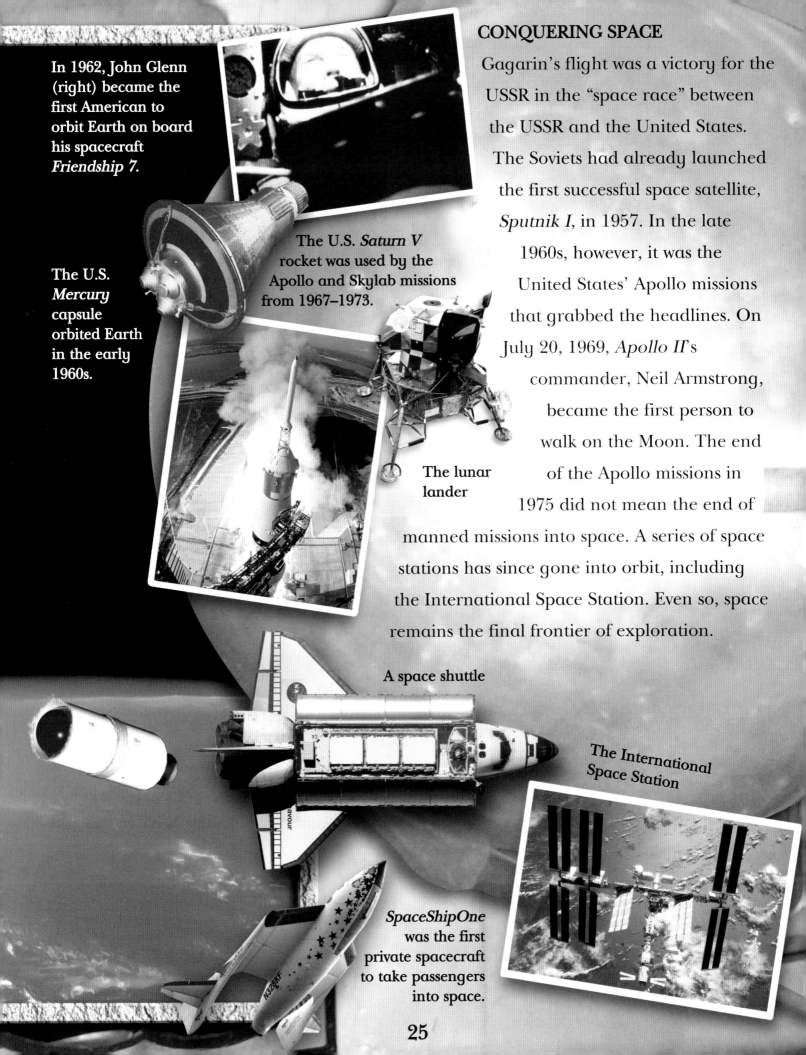

In 1962, John Glenn (right) became the first American to orbit Earth on board his spacecraft *Friendship 7*.

The U.S. *Mercury* capsule orbited Earth in the early 1960s.

The U.S. *Saturn V* rocket was used by the Apollo and Skylab missions from 1967–1973.

The lunar lander

CONQUERING SPACE

Gagarin's flight was a victory for the USSR in the "space race" between the USSR and the United States. The Soviets had already launched the first successful space satellite, *Sputnik I*, in 1957. In the late 1960s, however, it was the United States' Apollo missions that grabbed the headlines. On July 20, 1969, *Apollo II*'s commander, Neil Armstrong, became the first person to walk on the Moon. The end of the Apollo missions in 1975 did not mean the end of manned missions into space. A series of space stations has since gone into orbit, including the International Space Station. Even so, space remains the final frontier of exploration.

A space shuttle

The International Space Station

SpaceShipOne was the first private spacecraft to take passengers into space.

The Best of the Rest

JOHN CABOT
(1450–1498)

Five years after Columbus, Italian-born navigator John Cabot also tried to reach Asia by sailing west. After spending time trading in the Mediterranean, he moved to Bristol, the

John Cabot dressed in the typical costume of Venice, Italy

second-largest seaport in England. He won the support of King Henry VII of England for his expedition. Cabot left England in May 1497 and reached the coast of Canada on June 24. It is said he landed in and named Newfoundland, although Cape Bonavista is officially recognized as his landing place. He became the first European to land in North America since the Vikings, almost 500 years before. He returned to England convinced, however, that he had found the coast of China. He was made an admiral and set off on another voyage in 1498. However, he and his crew were never heard from again.

AMERIGO VESPUCCI
(1451–1512)

Navigator and explorer Amerigo Vespucci was born in Florence, Italy. He worked for the famous de Medici family, who sent him to Seville, Spain, in 1492. There, he met and became friends with Christopher Columbus. In 1499, Vespucci sailed for the second time across the Atlantic, joining a Spanish expedition that reached South America and the mouth of the Amazon River. The newly discovered continent of America is said to have been named after him. The name first appeared on a map in 1507.

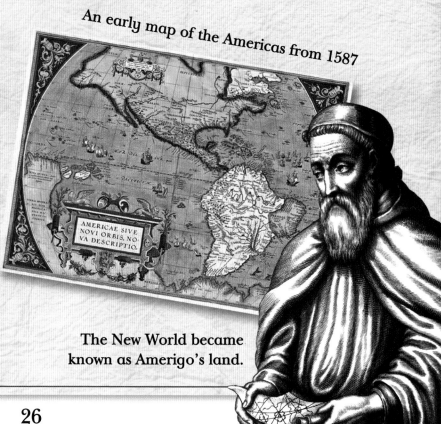

An early map of the Americas from 1587

The New World became known as Amerigo's land.

HERNÁN CORTÉS (1485–1547)

The son of a Spanish nobleman, Hernán Cortés studied law before setting off to seek his fortune in the New World. In 1504, he sailed to Santo Domingo (Dominican Republic), then moved to Cuba in 1511 and helped Diego Velázquez conquer the island. In 1519, he was appointed by Velázquez, now the governor of Cuba, to lead an expedition to Mexico. Rumors had reached the Spanish about the amazing treasures there. Within two years of his arrival, Cortés had brought the mighty Aztec Empire to a brutal end. The Aztec capital, Tenochtitlán, was captured after a three-month-long battle. Mexico City was built on its ruins. In 1521, the city became the center of New Spain and Cortés was appointed governor.

FERDINANDO CORTES
CAVATO DA VN ORIGINALE FATTO INAZI
CHE SI PORTASSI ALLA CONQVISTA DEL MESSICO

Cortés is famous as a *conquistador*, the Spanish word for "conqueror."

Aztec trophies like this were displayed in Spain.

FRANCIS DRAKE (1540–1596)

The English navigator Francis Drake gained fame and fortune raiding Spanish ships in the Caribbean Sea. In 1577, more than 50 years after Magellan's historic expedition, Queen Elizabeth I chose Drake to command a second circumnavigation of the globe. Drake set sail with five ships, including his flagship, the *Pelican*, later renamed the *Golden Hind*. Although the real reason for his voyage was to find treasure, he made several discoveries. Most importantly, he proved that South America was a continent and sailed further north up the West Coast of North America than any other explorer.

Labeled a pirate by the Spanish, Francis Drake was considered a hero by the English.

A map from the 1580s of Drake's voyage

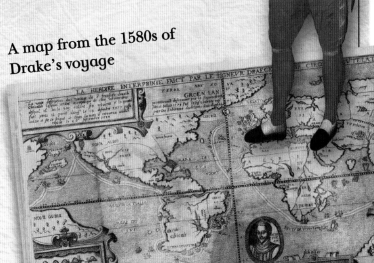

ALEXANDER VON HUMBOLDT (1769–1859)

One of the greatest scientific explorers, Baron Alexander von Humboldt, was born in Germany. From a young age, he was fascinated by nature and spent his time collecting plants, insects, and shells. In 1799, von Humboldt traveled to South America with French botanist Aime Bonpland. They spent five years there studying wildlife and geographical features, such as volcanoes and ocean currents. Back in Europe, their discoveries added greatly to the existing knowledge of science and geography.

A German statue in honor of Humboldt

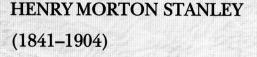

Humboldt was also a skilled botanical artist.

HENRY MORTON STANLEY (1841–1904)

Born in Wales, Stanley sailed to the United States as a ship's cabin boy in 1859. He fought in the American Civil War, then became a newspaper reporter, traveling across the United States, Asia, and North Africa. In 1870, the *New York Herald* sent Stanley to Africa to find David Livingstone, a British explorer, who was thought to be dead. After a dangerous 700-mile (1,125 km) expedition, he found Livingstone alive. Stanley returned to Africa several times and, in 1874, led an expedition to explore the Congo River that took three years and cost more than 200 lives.

Stanley was a fearless explorer.

Stanley is said to have greeted Livingstone with the words, "Dr. Livingstone, I presume?"

ROALD AMUNDSEN (1872–1928)

Roald Amundsen, a Norwegian doctor, gave up his medical studies to become one of the greatest polar explorers of all time. From 1903–1906, he sailed his ship, the *Gjoa*, through the Northwest Passage, becoming the first to navigate this waterway. His next expedition took him to Antarctica. In December 1911, he famously led the first team to reach the South Pole, beating Britain's Captain Scott by a month. Scott died on the return journey. From 1925–1926, Amundsen explored the Arctic by air and made the first trans-Arctic flight across the North Pole, in the airship *Norge*. He was killed in a plane crash while searching for survivors of another airship disaster in June 1928.

Amundsen was one of the greatest polar explorers.

Amundsen's Antarctic expedition ship, *Fram*

JACQUES-YVES COUSTEAU (1910–1997)

Born in France in 1910, Jacques-Yves Cousteau joined the French Navy when he was 20 years old. In 1943, he and the engineer Emile Gagnan developed the aqualung, a piece of equipment that revolutionized diving. For the first time, divers could carry their own air supply in cylinders on their backs, allowing them much greater freedom to explore the underwater world.

A diver wearing an aqualung

Cousteau also championed marine conservation, which is a hot topic today.

Timeline of Major Explorations

		The Places	The Explorers
ANCIENT	68,000 B.C.	WORLDWIDE	*Homo sapiens*
	300s B.C.	ATLANTIC OCEAN	Pytheas (Greece)
MODERN/MEDIEVAL ERAS	A.D. 1000	NORTH AMERICA	Leif Eriksson (Norway)
	1271–1295	CHINA	**Marco Polo (Italy)**
	1492	WEST INDIES	**Christopher Columbus (Italy/Spain)**
	1497	NORTH AMERICA	John Cabot (Italy/Britain)
	1497	INDIA	**Vasco da Gama (Portugal)**
	1499	SOUTH AMERICA	Amerigo Vespucci (Italy)
	1519	MEXICO	Hernán Cortés (Spain)
	1519–1521	AROUND THE WORLD	**Ferdinand Magellan (Portugal/Spain)**
	1620	UNITED STATES	**The Pilgrims (Britain)**
	1768	PACIFIC OCEAN	**James Cook (Britain)**
	1835	GALÁPAGOS ISLANDS	**Charles Darwin (Britain)**
20TH CENTURY	1919	ATLANTIC OCEAN	**Alcock and Brown (Britain)**
	1943	UNDERWATER	Jacques-Yves Cousteau (France)
	1961	SPACE	**Yuri Gagarin (Russia)**

The Results

The ancestors of early humans migrated from Africa to the Middle East, Asia, Australia, and Europe.

Sailed around the coast of Britain and wrote the first account of how people in Britain lived.

Sailed across the Atlantic and discovered Vinland (Newfoundland, Canada).

One of the first Europeans to explore China.

Sailed across the Atlantic and "discovered" the New World of the Americas.

The first European to reach North America (Newfoundland) after the Vikings.

The first European to sail around Africa and reach India by sea.

Reached the coast of South America and the mouth of the Amazon River.

Led an expedition to Mexico and brought the mighty Aztec Empire to an end.

First circumnavigational expedition; located the Magellanic Straits.

Sailed on the *Mayflower* from England and founded the Plymouth Colony on the East Coast of America.

Led three ground-breaking expeditions to explore and chart the Pacific Ocean.

Made many discoveries about the islands' unique wildife that helped him formulate his theory of evolution.

The first to fly across the Atlantic in less than 72 hours, showing that long-distance flight was possible.

Coinvented the SCUBA, enabling underwater exploration to take place.

On April 12, became the first person to fly in space in the *Vostok I* spacecraft.

Glossary

biplanes (BY-playnz) A type of aeroplane with two sets of wings, one above the other.

chronometer (kruh-NAH-meh-ter) A timepiece used at sea.

circumference (ser-CUM-frents) The distance around an object.

civilizations (sih-vih-lih-ZAY-shunz) A human society that is advanced and highly organized.

colony (KAH-luh-nee) A community formed by settlers in a country away from their homeland.

cosmonaut (KOZ-muh-naht) A Russian astronaut.

dowel (DOW-el) A thin, straight, wooden stick.

evolved (ih-VOLVD) Developed or gradually changed over a long period of time.

hominid (HAH-muh-nid) Any of the various groups of early people.

migration (my-GRAY-shun) A long journey from one place or country to another.

naturalist (NA-chuh-ruh-list) A person who studies the natural world.

pioneers (py-uh-NEERZ) People who explore or settle in new places, or develop something new.

Puritans (PYUR-ih-tenz) Very strict English Protestants (Christians) in the sixteenth and 17th centuries.

scurvy (SKUR-vee) A disease caused by a lack of vitamin C.

Index

Web Sites

Due to the changing nature of Internet links, PowerKids Press has developed an online list of Web sites related to the subject of this book. This site is updated regularly. Please use this link to access the list:
www.powerkidslinks.com/topt/explore/